Ode to the Viaduct
A Collection of Poems

Catherine Marie Abberton

Published in 2023 by FeedARead.com
Publishing.

A CIP catalogue record for this title is
available from the British Library.

For Peter, Mary, Sarah and Ben
With love

Preface

In Spring 2020, we were well into lockdown. Although work carried on for key workers, we still had our quiet times, as did the rest of the country. It was during this time that I sat down and penned Ode to the Viaduct. Once finished, I found myself writing more poems on themes connected with covid. Then, searching old files and diaries for previously written poems, I formed this collection.

Other sectors where my interest in poems and poets are prevalent include the following: When I was 11 years old, I entered a radio competition where I wrote and read a poem on air about the moon landing. (I didn't win.) And as a teenager, my English teacher, Mrs Williams expanded my interest in poetry with the introduction of different poets, types of poems and varied assignments. So, when taking a Psychology class where we had to keep a mood diary, I used poetry, music and colour as my mediums.

However, because I now have a collection of poems, I thought they would be best presented in book form. Reader, I hope that with the variety of themes, you can choose a favourite.

Contents

Nature 1

Dawn Chorus

Before the break of dawn in Spring
Migrate or breed, the reason for stirring
Hear the congregation sing
A joyful melody.

Throughout greenwood, farmland
and garden
Chirping in waves as they awaken
A symphony suitable for Arden
Heavenly.

Days of Joy and Jubilation

The Easter Vigil flame is lit
Candles are shared with congregation.
Symbolizing darkness to light,
A Pascal commemoration.
Bells around the world are ringing
Alleluia chorus singing
Of Resurrection glory.
Essential observances, too:
Fasting, feasts, traditions wholly
Encompassing spirits renewed.
Individuals reflecting.
Harmony projecting.
Rejoice and blossom like Hyacinths!
Or Iris whose fragrance is spread.
Or Dogwood whose legend's a labyrinth
Of crooked branches and petals tipped-red.
Greetings as fresh as morning dew:
'Happy Easter to you…. and to you!'
Family gatherings are planned.
Baskets of eggs distributed.
Chicks and bunnies and little lambs,
Water and pastel colours contributed
To days of joy and jubilation.

O Tree, O Tree

I stand in awe to see how from a seed
The mighty oak, white birch, chestnut or lime
Emerges. 'Tis quite a marvellous deed.
Nature provides soil, sun, water and time.
From root to base, then, layered stem with bark
Bridging branches bearing leaves for canopy
Lone standing, on plantations or in parks,
Trees present sylvan splendour majesty.
With change of seasons, flowers and fruit flourish.
Trees provide a natural home for fauna.
With harvested fruit and berries, we're nourished.
From ancient times, they're symbols of honour.

To the Farmer of Sheep
(Inspired on walks with our children)

I walk in leisure to your gate
Pausing to encompass
The landscape that is your backdrop.
Wonder in abundance!

Lush green fields encased by stonewalls
That separate and protect
Far-reaching views of uplands
Trees and beck add effect.

Through pasture, passed paddock and pen
Sheep graze in the still calm
As flocks gather as friends, their
Families keep the farm.

I know you sacrifice greatly
You are so dedicated
To ewe and tup and gimmer
As chores are delegated.

Are you vexed to know I pass through
In freedom, too delighted?
Do you know I yearn to farm but it's
A love unrequited?

At trail's end, I raise an invocation
For all who labour here.
In turn, the venture lingers,
In heart and mind held near.

Summer At Its Best

Dawn chorus beckons
The sun rising, early.
Flowers are blossoming
Colourful and pearly.
Blue sky and sunshine
Fill one with joy,
Long summer holidays
Hours to enjoy.
Butterflies, ladybirds
Glow-worms and starfish,
Picnics and barbeques
Fresh fruits that nourish.
Long-drawn days in the sun
Wearing lotion and hats,
Time spent with relatives
Playing games, having chats.
Bare feet in the sand
Frisbee on the beach
Slides at waterparks
Rainbow's end out of reach.
Collect shells and memories
Relax, read and rest
Music in the park
Summer at its best!

Au Revoir to Summer
for Pennie

Sirius shines bright
Fading through daylight;
North-easterlies clear skies,
Dog days demise.
Seasons in transition:
Birds await migration,
Creatures heed signs
As nature realigns.
Summer flowers wither
Making way for heather.
Deciduous trees
Soon to lose their leaves.
Landscapes emit ambience;
Sunsets beam radiance.
Early evenings drawn,
Harvest season dawns;
Scents of spice, like incense
Entice earth's recompense.
Harvest moon soon to rise
Illuminating the sky.
Halcyon days imprimatur
Ennobles departure.
Summer is replaced,
Autumn is embraced.

Autumn

Slight essence of Spring, Summer wanes
Equinox means Winter refrains
                     Come Autumn

Breathe the terrene scent of autumn
As the once fruited plants succumb
                     Crisp and earthy

Envision leaves crimson and golden
Set free as trees no longer hold them
                     Feuille morte

Bearded tooth and dead man's finger
Amethyst deceiver come to linger
                     Mushrooms vary

As squirrels gather, hedgehogs gorge
Badgers, fox and dormouse forage
                     Nuts and berries

Spider lilies and goldenrods
Shrinking iris, berries in pods
                     Ornate foliage

Swallows migrate, swifts are hawking
Partridges run, pheasants squawking
                     Goldcrests in hedge

Plumbs and blackberries to harvest
Pumpkins, squash, spinach and parsnip
                    Hot apple cider

Collect conkers, make a scarecrow
Find pine cones under the conifer
                    Mind the spiders

Corn mazes, hayrides and football
Diwali, stargazing at nightfall
                    Constellations

A time for thanksgiving and prayer
Family, friends, all those whose lives we
share
                    Uniting nations

Slight essence of Spring, Summer wanes
Equinox means Winter refrains
                    Welcome Autumn

(First read in public at Sasha Tiffany's
Yoga Class 28 Sept 2020)

The Dove

Not unlike any other bird
Round form, short legs, small head
A dove is white or grey or tan,
Bill of pinkish-red.
And with large wings that whistle when
In flight, they are spread.

Gliding, streaming, floating freely
Wayfinder in the sky,
Balance between earth and heaven
Guise of gentle guide.
Peace and serenity are graces
The dove signifies.

As messenger or oracle
Portrayed in written word,
Infers a link with Higher Power,
This holy sprite, this bird.
Symbol dovetailing cultures and
Peace throughout the world.

December

Let me keep this winter image
Etched upon my heart
This be such a tangible gift
Of the Creator's art.

See the beauty of the fresh, crisp
White blanketing of snow
Settling flora and fauna in their
Dormant state, below.

Look on the horizon, there's a
Ribbon of pale pastel
Colours of cream, aqua, dove-grey
More snow, the heavens compel.

The spectre of the cloud-clad sun
In time illuminates
The portrayal of the season
And the feasts we celebrate.

The pine trees, holly and ivy
And stable are allegorical
Ergo, the reason for gift-giving
Started by the Oracle.

Thus, seek and share endowments
Sage or ordinary folk
These are gifts and blessings to gain
As chronicles evoke.

Save this semblance of serenity
Release any unrest
Illustrate one's own benevolence
Through each new year's quest.

Lore 2

The Legend of the White Birch Trees

There is a town in Penns Woods named
Vandenhoek.

It prospered from a coal town, with the
help of all the local folk

Who equipped it with utilities of modern
day.

Yet, 'It's a nice place to visit but....' many
people say.

Finding out the reasons 'why' was not a
hard task.

It seems the opinion was the same of all
who were asked.

Of all the pains that irked them most, there
were two

That prompted ill feelings, of which, there
was nothing they could do.

The first of these was not uncommon to
these folks,

Since they realised its birth in the growth
of Vanderhoek.

Seems the rulers of the town became quite unjust

For this reason, the rulers, by the angered folks were cussed.

The second reason aroused discussion of such

That the hearts of many people were united.

It began with the plight where the folks did their best

To save the ten white birch trees that were growing in the West.

High upon a little hill, in the west of town,

There stood the ten white birch tree, that's all that could be found.

Here, they welcomed a precious oak tree. Aware

Of its presence, they let its branches intertwine with theirs.

The tallest of the trees stood stern but
flexible

Near a pair whose separation would be
next to impossible.

Another white birch seemed to be quite
militant

Standing by a bashful tree that refused to
be flippant.

Two saplings were competing with each
other there

By another youthful tree, who'd not a
single care.

The last two trees portrayed beauty and
strength, but all

Were humbled to the Son, being
ecclesiastical.

Ten white birches plus a precious oak,
united

Dusk's silhouette would lose its grace, if
the uninvited

Would venture in and steal the life

Of the innocent trees, causing the lot,
much pain and strife.

The town folk stood helpless when the machines drew near.

They wished to defend the trees but would not because of fear.

Each feared what would happen if they questioned the law

They even feared each other and that was their greatest flaw.

An axe was raised to the sky, ready to strike

When a stranger stepped forward because he did dislike

What was about to happen. It was he who shouted, 'Stop!!'

With a thunderous voice that was heard throughout the mountain top.

'Take one good look at your village below. It lacks

The presence of the very tree you now prepare to axe!'

The rulers, they ignored the man, but the town folk

They agreed; they must defend the birches of Vandenhoek.

The rulers saw that the town folk weren't on their side

So, they tried to think of something, so with them they'd abide.

'Look at your modern city, city of concrete....

Buildings, pavements, streets and more. We'll make it all complete.

The town folk grew angrier to see how they let

The rulers form a concrete city, so, with much regret

They turned to the stranger asking what they should do.

'Let them destroy or make them rebuild. It's all up to you.'

'Now, it seems to me this town's been ignorant

To the lives the white birch lead. They try hard to be gallant.

They try hard to succeed. Defend them. Do
no less.

Attend and preserve them; they're a
mighty fortress.'

'I advise a park filled with nature's
monuments:

Trees and plants and animals. Never raise a
fence.

Fill it with reminders of visions of the past.

Safeguard and conserve it so, forevermore
it lasts.

Working together, a park was raised,
composed

Of trees, plants and animals for activity or
repose.

This did not complete their duties, they
will finish

When unjust laws and actions of rulers will
diminish.

And what of the stranger, who bravely
shouted, 'Stop!'

And told the people how to preserve the
mountaintop?

Those without faith say he was just another
guy.

But others believe he was the *spirit* of days
gone by.

(1976)

Ode to the Viaduct

From a distance, it holds its grandeur still.
Combined columns of brick and stone, bridging
Upland pastures, sylvan vales and ghyll.
What joy marks such monumental ridging!
What pride due to those whose design and skill
Brawn and zeal created such lodestar!
Seventeen arches spanning a quarter mile
Base, parapet and deck whose track fills
The desire of adventurer and rover
To pause here and linger for a while.

The trackway bestows a portal of keen
Terrestrial splendour. Gaze at the landscape;
Study the wilds. Trees, bush and shrub akin
Abode of birds, butterflies, wildlife and wape*.

Part of the Great Northern Railway Trail,
Time was when the trains carried freight
and travellers.
Now blessed be its province as pathway
For walkers, runners and cyclists, it
unveils.
Honour Fraser, Johnson, Benton and
Woodiwiss,
Jackson and Manywells for this noble
trailway.

The viaduct extends itself to friend,
Family and nature as an apex,
An apogee, here with to inter-blend.
Senses allured by Creator's effects:
:
Champion the children
The runners and ramblers
Reservoir walkers
And Hewenden anglers.
Hail the horse riders
Eye the drone flyers
Mind cyclists and skaters
And skating board acers
Birdwatchers avid
Picnickers pleased
Bubble blowers, too
Climbers of trees,

*Babies in buggies
And piggyback riders
Along come scooters and hoverboard
gliders
Dog-walkers stroll, berry-pickers reap.*

And should the flow cease
A godsend for solitude and peace.

*Wape: New Guinea, a human being, in
contrast to a spirit being

Yallah! Yallah!
(A sea shanty)

With a backdrop of war and hunger
Loyal to grandfathers' trade, the younger
Set sail to fish and wonder
Will this day bring luck or hardship?

Will this day bring luck or
hardship?
Sailing on our fishing boats
Overworked and weary
Favour, we're denied.

Years of conflict, lives lost and vessels
Restrictions made fishing unsuccessful.
Duties loom, companions nestle
With friends whose boats are ill-equipped
.
Fuel, engines and nets are scarce, too
Raiders steal boats to smuggle arms
through.
The cost of war ensues.
Will this day bring luck or hardship?

Will this day bring luck or
hardship?
Sailing on our fishing boats
Overworked and weary
Favour, we're denied

Fishermen from Yemen in the
Gulf of Aden
Wish tuna, sardines and lobsters would
laden
Their boats, to trade in
For a fair wage from week long trips.

Yallah! Yallah! A whale is in sight!
Lifeless, yet still it shows it's might.
The fleet of fishermen unite
Will this day bring luck or hardship?

Will this day bring luck or
hardship?
Sailing on our fishing boats
Overworked and weary
Favour, we're denied.

Through the faecal odour, pungent and
strong
The whale is hooked and pulled along.
A treasure within belongs
To those who excavate the mammal crypt.

Ambergris! Ambergris! Formed inside the
whale.
Waxy, black, rock-like, descaled.
Treasure of the Sea prevails.
Will this day bring luck or hardship?

> Will this day bring luck or
> hardship!
> Sailing on our fishing boats
> Overworked and wear
> Favour, we're denied.

Floating gold worth millions when oil is
extracted
From the cyst it had impacted.
The fishermen reacted
By giving thanks and praise in worship.

Ambergris, this precious catch, is used in making scents
And medicines in the Orient.
Gross domestic product to augment.
Indeed, this day will bring good luck, not hardship!

> This day will bring good luck
> not hardship!
> Sailing on our fishing boats
> Overworked and weary
> Favour is implied!

The fishermen with villagers,
 shared the net.
Then, back to work with no regrets
Knowing it was kismet.
Will **this** day bring luck or hardship!

> Will this day bring luck or
> hardship?
> Sailing on our fishing boats
> Overworked and weary
> Favour will preside.

The Fisherman

…..and throughout the years to come
Christ called more fisherman
To cast their nets in still waters
And to work together with others
That they may oversee millions
To be thankful for their gain
And to find enlightenment in the words:
"Come after me, I will make you fishers of
men."

I met a fisherman the other day
He was both friendly and serene
He held much grace that flowed
so deep within
That it wasn't left unseen.

I watched him live each minute
of the day
Letting no chore be left undone
Offering his deeds to the One
he truly loved
The Spirit, Father and the Son.

'Twas so impressive just to
watch him reach
Through words and actions,
many he would teach
Like when an urchin 'neath a
reef was caught
With credence less than should
have been
He snatched it with his net, gave
absolution,
Then, 'twas set in
Stilled waters, nearer kin.

Not just to love afresh on
golden pond
But to express good news
each day
And too, to let others know
There's still a chance
if they lose way
Through words and actions,
many we could reach,
When our profession of faith
we teach.

Praise 3

Happy Father's Day

Happy the children whose father is patient.
Happy the child whose father is wise.
Happy the children whose father
Finds Truth in the teachings
Of science and music and maths.
Your constant love for your children,
Reaches the skies.

Your constant love for your children
To the heavens enfolds
As the love from your children
Is the greatest gift to behold.

Behold the child:
Who fills the days
With love and laughter
Who has a smile that brings
Warmth to the soul
Who is content.

She is precious in thine eyes
Joy and beauty are round about her
Faith and courage are the foundations of
her future.
She is yours to cherish.
You are her first love.

The essence of your children
Is a reflection of your wisdom and humour
And love.

To The Father Of Our Children

Words cannot express
The gratitude within my being

For inception of a progeny
So unique

For the constant care and counsel
For understanding and patience

They thrive
Formed from a sound foundation
Secure in faith and hope for a
Blissful future.

An Anniversary Poem

When love was new
To me and you
It grew and grew as these things do
How I loved you!

A family
Together, we made joyfully
And skilfully
Too, playfully.

What awesome wond'rings
The future brings:
Time for sharing
Caring, loving
Enduring, securing…

Happy Anniversary of our wedding.

Anniversary Poem
(for Jim and Elizabeth on their 50th
Wedding Anniversary)

Some friendships can blossom and flourish
Through the graces and blessings that
Nourish appreciation in time.

Some friendships are created
Transforming one's spirit
With favour and
Influenced by the Divine.

This friendship has featured in years of
Celebrations and aspirations for a future
Of love, harmony, health and
Good cheer!

Valiant 4

SOJOURNER

His namesake is Poland's patron
He doesn't stay, nor does he run,
He came forth proclaiming puissance,
being bold
Then, once obtained, in check he did not
hold.
Early years brought profound education
Thus, he taught in time of maturation,
Embracing dexterous abilities,
An artificer of facilities,
With internship being less than regale
As a practitioner, he did not fail.
Ergo, he chose a woman and married,
Then, together, nine children, they carried.
Wisdom and experience, soon had rolled
To a philosopher – avant-garde mould.
Hence, with faith held steadfast,
he still sojourns
And continues to share, all that he learns.

Pathfinder
for Peter

Whilst, we are companions
There's something you should know
Paths are crossed for reasons
Like ours so long ago
O noble pathfinder
What joy you brought to me
Counsellor and educator
Were allied in unity
To traverse and explore
Footpaths and thoroughfares
In grand and great outdoors
Free to stroll anywhere.

Untraceable, your lead
To see nature's delights
Through valley we'd proceed
To hill of distinct heights
Pathfinder turned parent
Guide to a path of creed
With virtues inherent
With hopes they will succeed
And still, we trek the trails
Of woodland and of field
We talk and we share tales
Future plans revealed.

There are some folks that need
Your sense of inception
From troubles they are freed
Given your direction
Your avant-garde approach
Makes paths where none exist
You give more time than most
To find the path that's easiest
Still, we have miles to go
Together, down the roads
Where they end, we don't know.
But with blessings, we're bestowed.

Contemplation

When I stand high on Baildon Moor
I see far more than fields and farms below.
For in the West, there dwells a family, core
Of my being, formed of my being; they
grow.
They grow with values of faith
Hard work instilled
Provide good humour and music
and more, the four.
As those before
Who came to work the mills,
We struggle, we strive, we love, we
endure.

When I stand high on Baildon Moor
I see far more than fields and farms below.
I see how the realms of Deity are stored
Within us. When inspired,
We let graces flow.
'Tis faith that binds us to the future.
Inner strength, I pray that we be given.
And wisdom to lead our children on paths
whilst
We're providing for them
A good living.

Flickerings

"All the questions I ask
In this mission to cope
Do I pay, in the task,
A premium on Hope?"

What of love…..what of love
Unconditional be.
When enkindled by Jove
Is undaunted and free?

If the flame burns no brighter
It at least preservers
In good faith I hold tighter
'Til the omniscient one nears.

One Man's Peace
(for Peter)

Let England boast of him who plays and
then
Teaches of matter, motion, heat and light.
Of Flickerings and lambs he chose to
write.
He holds so deep a Spirit bound within,
With thoughts that might form a character
for Rodin.
The search for justice is his plight,
If all the wrong we could set right:
Then peace would be his gift to animal
and man.
But peace is just a vision still.
Where does he find release?
With Chopin, dancing or his barley's fill.
So until private wars within will cease,
'Til serenity is held as each man's will,
This can be but one man's peace.

The Poet

From daylight to dusk
The old man, he writes
Retired and grey
'Tis death whom he fights.

Many years ago
When he was a youth,
He would write poems
Of honour and truth,
Of love and people,
And animals, too.
He found writing poems
Was easy to do.

It was at this time
Hardly more than a child
Spoke to his pa
Who became riled:
"No son of mine will
Sit around writing
With war going on, you should be
fighting!"

The boy, he did join
The service because
The patriotic
citizen does.

The poet, he vowed
That he would return
To write of his life
And all that he learned.

So, for hours, he writes
No grudge does he hold.
Without his experience
Less stories be told.

Plight 5

Rescue boats beckoned
They pray they will be welcomed
One looks like papa

Headlines shout: BE GONE

But you don't know their history

They've looked Death in the eye

Integrity (redefined)

Instilled with ethics:
Principles, Creed, Honesty and Coalition
But with short-comings!

*with reference to travel and parties
during covid restrictions

The Arrangement

We
Are bonded, sister cousin, by
Bangles, and rings that hold
Us to commitment.

Should
One peer beneath the veils and
Scarfs that both protect and disguise our
emotion
They'd find hurt and unhappiness.

Leave
The riddles and labyrinths
Of our relationships that
We may be free.

Tomorrow
Holds a promise of contentment and bliss.

Infusion*

How good it is to walk
In the fields and the woods.
The aromatic flowers and trees
Refreshes our senses.
We have attentive interest in flora and
fellow creatures.
You bring such happiness.

Oh, Mother Nature

Satisfy our intrigue
how this virus to restrain.
Share the element we need
to use as a vaccine.
Surely the joy you bring to us
resembles what we share.
We trust you'll secure this destine.

Dear Earth Mother

*Lockdown 2020

Hereafter

Occurring in summer, during
Covid, twenty-twenty
And with all the hardship present,
Added adversity
Came with a blast in Beirut
Which brought forth May's publicity.

But we've wandered many a weary foot

Upon returning to her home,
May Abboud Melki played
A folk song and Arabic hymns
On her piano left unscathed.
Volunteers and family paused,
Her granddaughter, amazed.

And there's a hand my trusty friend!

'Twas shared on social media:
Woman beset with debris noted.

May-Lee, May's granddaughter
'beauty from ashes' caption wrote.

'…pushed through pain, for a few
moments peace',
A news report quote.

Since auld lang syne

And playing on, Arabic hymns
After Auld Lang Syne
Offering hope for community and
Family intertwined.
A strong message May entrusted
Lean into love Divine.

And we'll take a cup of kindness yet
For auld lang syne.

Eternal 6

Morning Prayer

Awaken my soul

That I may give thanks to the Great Spirit
For this day.

Open my mind's eye that I may see
The mission set before me.

Nourish me with sustenance for body and
spirit.
Grant that I will use
my eyes to see those who require my
attention
my ears to hear their call
my words to encourage
my smile to uplift
my arms to comfort
my hands to restore.

And at days end, let me feel content
to know that I have brought joy
to those whose paths I crossed
and delighted my deity.

Vocation Prayer

I believe
Father,
You will be done
As revealed to me.

Christ Jesus
Through your teachings
Guide me as I carry out
The duties of my vocation.

Holy Spirit
Escort me on the path
Of a faithful life.

Amen.

She will be remembered

In the quiet moments.

She will live in the hearts of everyone who
loved her.

In the seeds of this life,
We find hope in a better life to come.

On the death of Leo's infant granddaughter

Kizito

I did not know you
But I feel sorrow on your passing.
You left an imprint on my daughter's
being
As your paths were crossing.
I pray you send comfort and healing
To those who are here grieving.

19-09-20

Our Farewell

United here, mournful and grieved
With sympathy we can console
We can listen, share our stories
As we salute our kindred soul.

A man of word, a man of song
Was always there to lend a hand
Strong work ethic, dedicated
Faithful friend and family man.

Let this be our farewell, to companion and
colleague
We were privileged and honoured to know
He'll be remembered for his acts of
kindness
    Rest in peace
    Rest in peace

We'll keep him close in memory
Cherish thoughts of happier days
Support, inspire, persevere, be loyal
Celebrate life, his legacy.

Let this be our farewell, to companion and
colleague
We were privileged and honoured to know
He'll be remembered for his acts of
kindness
    Rest in peace
    Rest in peace.

Tribute to Len Wilson

The Last Farewell

We are gathered here to say farewell to our
friend
We'll miss him, he was quite the
gentleman.
We are left to feel downhearted in his
passing
And now we'd like to share our sentiment.
He would not want us to linger in
bereavement
There's still so much on earth we need to
do.

Farewell to you, dear friend,
We are grateful for your guidance as
compeer and as a family man.

You were pleased to live most of your life
in Yorkshire
Settling in East Morton near the church
and school.
A Steeton Male Voice Choir endorser
St Luke's is where you'd also sing a tune.

With family and friends, so much
achievement.
Starting with a dance and a girl you did
pursue.

Farewell to you, dear friend,
You were so reliant as our compere
and as a family man.

Your strong work ethic we need to
continue
In the choir and in community,
In church and school. We owe it to our
children.
We know there is much opportunity.
Then, let this be your legacy to Steeton
And all who were your friends along
the way.

Farewell to you, dear friend
You were dedicated as compadre
and as a family man.

7-4-21

New World Symphony

As we assembled outside in our bubbles
The service began with one of Dvorak's
pieces.
We weren't allowed to enter the chantry.
Peace rendered itself through the tannoy
And swathed the mourners.

The vicar read her life's story
Composed by the family.
As he read, he recounted her life and
He encouraged us to allow ourselves
To feel sorrow or delight in viewing her
past.

*…was born… went to school at… teaching
degree…church-goer…. met the man who
was to be her husband and together raised
a son.*

A woman left her bubble to console
another mourner.

*… arts and crafts… sewing…
baking… well-travelled.*

Some of the words were swept away
on a breeze or distance or on our own
thoughts.

...Grade 8 in piano. (We didn't know this.
She never said.)
... loved to work with the SEN children.
In retirement, enjoyed going out to eat with
past colleagues.
 (We enjoyed linking up for a catch up.)

The vicar said we'll pause for
Our own individual thoughts of
commiseration:
She reminded me of my own mother at
times.
She often used enhanced facial expressions
when telling a story.

An usher declared:
The family is coming out,

Come closer.
Everyone moved only slightly nearer
Respecting social distancing.

After a few words with her husband,
we saw her son and his partner at a
distance.
(Their wedding was postponed because of
covid.)

And so it ended.

Quintessence of Harmony
Human symphony

Going Home
New world sympathy

(Attended August 2020 during Lockdown)

Too Much

Is it asking too much
For a kind word,
A bit of fairness
Or a smile.

Is it asking too much
For some company
For conversation
Or a shared joke.

Actually, it is a lot to ask
But it doesn't really matter
I just thought I knew you better.
I just thought you could be my Anam Cara.

.

SAT NAM

My soul
delights

in the formulae
of physics

the essence
of nature and

the constant
heartbeat

that encircles
myself and the divine.

Epitaph

To you who linger at my resting place
This stone is well worth reading
If you feel a sense of serenity
That is because my request
To the Creator is to bless you
With such grace.

If when my body's buried
And heaven calls not for me
Just let my soul be carried
On Yorkshire winds and I'll roam free
I'll wander in good company.

"Scarlet as heather, your soul"
Was the perpetual din
But that was never the goal
To be guilty of seven sins
"I've been sinned against, not sinned."

So not worthy of heaven
Let my limbus soul then be
Set sail on the wind, as guardian
O'er Yorkshire Moors for sheep
and sheep again
Mesolithic souls, who Christian
Could have been.

I'll fly where kingfishers fly
Where breathless beauty pours forth
I'll fly with rare butterflies
There upon the Yorkshire Moors
My soul journey through northern skies
Here, my heaven lies.

So when my bones are buried
My spirit needs a haven
Perpetual yet varied
Then, let Yorkshire be my heaven
…….and all will be forgiven.

Pupils 7

Soap, Schoolwork and Laughter
(Year 5 Class '20)

When C - O - V - I - D came,
We couldn't go to school.
We'd lessons in our own home,
So that was pretty cool.

Fast forward to September.
Now we're in Year 5!
We're back in class at St Joe's,
And this is how we thrive:

We've formed ourselves a bubble.
It's invisible; it's clear.
It fits some thirty children
And staff who persevere.

Each day we wash our hands as
We enter with our peers.
Our desks are side by side now.
New rules. You must not sneer!

A prayer to start each morning.
The timetable's the same.
We're told in Maths, we're awesome.
Results we can explain.

We've formed ourselves a bubble
It's invisible; it's clear.
It fits some thirty children
And staff who persevere.

We have a break for fresh air,
too, mingle with our mates.
Then, back in class for English.
some poems we create.

We know that we are special.
We know that we are unique.
Our teachers often tell us.
(Sometimes, we give them cheek.)

We've formed ourselves a bubble
It's invisible; it's clear.
It fits some thirty children
And staff who persevere.

We try our best all morning,
That's all our teachers ask.
We try to make good choices,
As we complete our tasks.

At quarter past, 'It's dinners!'
After a little play.
We still have many lesson
To finish off the day.

We've formed ourselves a bubble
It's invisible; it's clear.
It fits some thirty children
And staff who persevere.

We still have

    :Science

        Or History

Computing

        Or R.E.

Music

        Or Geography

Junior Jam

      Or P.E.

        SCARF   or DT.......

We're pleased to be in Year 5
We're here, ready to learn.
We know that that's important,
Tomorrow, we'll return.

We've formed ourselves a bubble
Made of soap, school work and laughter.
What we learn in 2020
We'll recall forever after!

With Thanks to EB & Rachel
And, also Thanks to LR

Post-cards from the Moon
For TS and Class

Year 1 are 'sending postcards from the
Moon'.
A space-ship had landed near boulders
and dunes.
Three astronauts in the Columbia module
landed the Eagle after 6 days of travel.
We're writing postcards on what we
have learned.
Armstrong, Aldrin and Collins confirmed
They were the first to explore this frontier.
Their contact to Earth was made clear:

'That's one small step for a Man,
one giant leap for Mankind.'
And with that, they left footprints behind.
They planted a flag to mark the occasion
Setting aspirations for the next generations
This happened in the summer of 1969
Now it's 2022 when,
our postcards we've designed.
Once the postcard arrives, look at the
stamp
It's of Laika, the space dog, a Soviet
champ.

We're Celebrating SAT's Week
(As requested for the Year 6 class)

We're celebrating SAT's Week
To show beyond a doubt
What we've learned since Reception
Is what it's all about.

Monday is SPAG, not Bolognese
But Grammar and Punctuation.
We'll also do our spelling
And not lose concentration.

Tuesday, we'll be reading sources
Then, answers, we will write.
Through comprehension and inference,
They will come to light.

Wednesday is Maths: Arithmetic
And Reasoning, relying
On strategies of Logic,
Techniques, we'll be applying

It's Maths again on Thursday.
We'll answer all the questions,
Using skill to solve each problem,
Just as we did in lessons.

We're celebration SAT's Week
After months of preparation.
'Good Luck!', high-fives and fist pumps,
All add to the occasion.

We're celebration SAT's Week
With a good night's sleep, less screen-time
Fresh air, play, a chat with parents
And a quiet word to the divine.

We're celebrating SAT's Week
With encouragement to friends,
Special thanks to teaching staff
As we're becoming living legends!

(Thanks to SL)

SAG

Ingram Content Group UK Ltd.
Milton Keynes UK
UKHW011957220523
422165UK00004B/61

9 781803 028132